What the Pencil Saw

Bianca Shaw

BookLeaf Publishing

Presentation by *BookLeaf Publishing*

Web: www.bookleafpub.com

E-mail: info@bookleafpub.com

ISBN: 9789357442107

First edition 2023

This book is dedicated to all the children in my life - Virginia, Samantha, Charlee, Jack, Wesley, Kennedy, Kate, Brady, Jonas, Sadie, Barrett, and all the other creative young minds who might pick this book up.

ACKNOWLEDGEMENT

Thank you to my family and Preston Parker for supporting my creative journey. A very special thank you to Vicky Tusken, Lori Dowd, Steve Whitman, and Paul Thill. Without you, I would not have a passion for the written word.

PREFACE

Someone once told me it was impossible to fly. But I fly in my dreams every night. This book is for anyone with an imagination and the courage to use it.

ALL ARE WELCOME

All are welcome
Inside my house
All are invited
From human to mouse

If you did not have hands
If you did not have feet
If you had no eyes
No nose
And no teeth

If you did not have hair
If you did not have cheeks
If you had pointy ears
A long neck
And a beak

It would not matter
You would matter the same
You would still be welcome
And I'd be glad you came

For my house has no windows
No paintings hung on the wall
You see - my house isn't a house
Not really at all

My house beats inside
This thing called my chest
My door is always open
And to my house, you're the best

PLAIN JANE

Plain Jane
Was always the same
Dressed in blue jeans
And white top every day

She watched the same shows
And ate the same food
Nothing new or exciting
Just the same plain old mood

One day she woke up
All in a huff
Sick and tired
Of the same plain old stuff

She saw her same clothes
Sitting out on her bed
When a bright, new idea
Popped into her head!

She put on purple tights
And a bright yellow skirt
Polka dot socks
And a pink princess shirt

She put on gloves
And sunglasses too
A hat with a feather
And mismatched shoes

She ate blueberry pancakes
With loads of whipped cream
Instead of watching TV
She drew and daydreamed

She felt something happen
Deep down inside
A smile on her face
A gleam in her eye

She realized she wanted
To try new things more
Now Plain Jane
Is not so plain anymore

COLOR OUTSIDE THE LINES

I can’t remember where I put it
I have not had it in so long
I used to have it though
Unless, of course, I’m wrong

I remember I had it when I was young
But lost it along the way
It used to be right there with me
I would use it every day

I know I had it with me
When I'd color outside the lines
Or when I’d play pretend
It all felt real in my mind

I’d draw cotton candy clouds
And color the grass pink
But adults told me grass is green
They told me what to think

As I grew up and older
I got this strange sensation
Maybe I’d be happier
If I never lost my imagination

SNOW DAY

I woke up this morning and rubbed my eyes
When I saw something glisten right outside
I raced to the window, and what did I see?
A snow-covered paradise waiting for me!

I ran down the stairs and saw countless snow piles
I skipped to the kitchen and saw my mom smile
Mom said I could ask my neighbor to play
Because school was canceled for a snow day!

I jumped and hooped and hollered and danced!
I dug through the closet to find my snow pants!
I grabbed my neighbor and my sled
And to the big hill, we started to head

We climbed and climbed up and upper
A whole day to play, before having supper
We reached the top, above the town
Now for the fun part, going down!

We hopped on our sleds and started to slide
Freshly fallen snow gave our sleds perfect glide
We zoomed and zipped and soared so fast
How I wished the fun could last and last

We built a snowman and a giant igloo
We laid on the ground and made snow angels too
We had a wild snowball fight
Hours vanished, and soon the sun dipped out of sight

We rushed back home, giggling all the way
We had so much fun, a perfect snow day
Our cheeks were cold, with a rosy glow
We topped the day off with hot cocoa

When you're having fun, time sure seems to fly
And days like this are rare to come by
But I must say, "This was the best day ever
Because you and I got to spend it together!"

NEVER PULL A PUPPY’S TAIL

Never pull a puppy's tail
Or he might cry, and he might wail
Or he might turn into a slimy snail
Or sprout wings and whiskers and prickly scales

He might grow hooves and gloopy globs
Or stripes and feathers and little door knobs
Or melt into a slobbery blob
Or he might grow kernels, like corn on the cob!

Or maybe the puppy would feel hurt and get sad
And if a puppy was sad, wouldn't you feel bad?

So never pull a puppy's tail
Or he might cry, and he might wail
Maybe he'd scream or maybe he'd shout
One thing I know for sure is you should never find out!

IMPORTANT MESSAGE

Doris
told Michelle
to tell Boris
to tell Danielle
to tell Gabby
to tell Denise
to tell Abby
to tell Bernice
to tell Chloe
to tell Pam
to tell Zoey
to tell Sam
to tell Dean
to tell Erin
to tell Eileen
to tell Karen
to tell Kurt
to tell Rick
to tell Burt
to tell Nick
to tell Bo
to tell Lily
to tell Joe
to tell Billy
to tell Mary
to tell Bree
to tell Gary
to tell me
to tell Drew
to tell Clancy
to tell you
to tell Nancy
to watch out for
that great big sign!
...but I guess she didn't get the message in time

PICKY PETUNIA

Picky Petunia hated lettuce and tuna
She wouldn't eat bars- not Clif, not Luna
She wouldn't touch cabbage or even a pickle
She hated bread - wheat, rye, pumpernickel

She wouldn't touch broccoli, figs or blueberries
She wouldn't eat carrots, beets, salmon, or cherries
She wouldn't eat peas or lima beans
She especially hated salty sardines

She wouldn't eat breakfast if it came zested or dressed
She wouldn't eat brunch if it had a crunch to digest
She wouldn't eat her snack if it came in a pack
Or lunch if it came in a bunch or a sack

She always refused to try anything twice
Especially if it had salt, sugar, or spice
But when she grew up, she gave food a second chance
From cauliflower and beans to baguettes from France

She tried peaches, avocado, pears, and beef jerky
Asparagus, apples, grapes, and tofurkey
She tried every food, yes, even tuna
Turns out she loved it all… and never even knew-a

DON'T TELL MY MOTHER

My mother said to clean my room
Or I might lose something that I love
In my mounds of clothing
Or under all my toys and stuff

And I hate that she was right
And please don’t tell my mother
I did lose something that I love...
I think I lost my brother!

I BOUGHT MYSELF A YO-YO

I bought myself a yo-yo
To learn some cool new tricks
I bought myself a soccer ball
To have something to kick
I bought myself a tub of slime
To make my ooey gooey day
I bought myself a dollhouse
So I could always play
I bought myself some candy
Because candy is so sweet
I bought myself some ice cream too
It's my favorite treat to eat
I bought myself a pack of cards
Just to carry around
I bought myself a music box
That twirls when it is wound
I bought myself some building blocks
So I could build tall towers
I bought myself an iPad
To watch videos for hours
And today it's raining really hard
And, ya know, it's kind of funny
I need to buy some rain boots
But I seem to be out of money

TOO MUCH SUGAR CAN MAKE YOU SICK

Tonight my parents had plans to go and see a show
But before they left the house, I heard my dad on the phone
My babysitter canceled, her car was stuck in the snow
Which meant they had no choice but to leave me home alone

They told me to lock the doors
Go to bed on time, no tricks
And not to eat too many sweets
because too much sugar can make you sick

They pulled out of the driveway
And like I was in a race
I grabbed every sweet in sight
And started to stuff my face

I ate lots of cookies, some brownies, and pies
Pudding and Jell-O and a big plate of fries
I ate custard, muffins, candy, and scones
12 scoops of ice cream in a fresh waffle cone

Creme brûlée, donuts, and a 6-layer cake
Croissants dipped in a Nutella milkshake
Chocolate chip pancakes with whipped cream, so sweet
Caramel and nougat and Rice Krispies Treats

My tummy was filled to the absolute brim
I laid down on the couch, feeling quite grim
Just then, I heard the garage door buzz
My parents walked in and asked how my night was

My tummy made a deep gurgling sound
My face turned green, my head started to pound
I covered my mouth and ran to the bathroom so quick
I guess too much sugar really can make you sick

WHAT DO YOU THINK?

Why does it rain?
Why does it snow?
Why is the sky blue?
Why does the wind blow?

Why can't animals talk?
Could they if they tried?
Why do birds fly?
And why can't I?

What is love?
And why do we feel it?
When I get hurt
How does my body heal it?

I think it rains
When the clouds are sad
I think it snows
When the sky is glad

Birds fly to see things from new heights
And I can fly too, in my dreams at night
I feel loved because I am, through and through
My body heals because it's meant to

There is so much
I do not know
But with my imagination
I can make it up as I go

When I grow up
Maybe I'll know things like why toots stink
But for now, I'm not sure
So, what do you think?

STICKY VICKY

Sticky Vicky blew bigger gum bubbles
Than anyone I knew
She was always chomp, chomp, chomping
Constant chew, chew, chew

One day she offered me a piece
Of her grape bubble gum
Out of all the times she chomped and chewed
She never offered me some

So I said, “Yes! Yes! Yes!”
Unwrapped it with glee
She warned, “Do not swallow it!"
I don’t know what came over me

Chomp! Chomp!
Chew! Chew!
“I bet I can blow
A bigger bubble than you!”

As I blew and blew and blew and blew
The bubble grew and grew and grew
It grew so big I could no longer see
Vicky right in front of me

It grew over my head
And over my roof
And I started to float
Far away in a poof!

I rose up to the clouds
Way up in the sky
Flew up past some birds
So I waved to them “Hi!”

I couldn’t let go
Or I’d fall to the ground
And on top of that
I was scared to look down

I floated so far
Past mountains and seas
I drifted away
Just riding the breeze

I saw China and London
Tokyo, Paris, and more
Drifted so far round the world
I ended up back at my door

I thought "Oh no!
Now I have to get down!"
So I sucked in the big bubble
As I floated down to the ground

Vicky was stunned
"Oh, what did you do?"
"I told you I could blow
A bigger bubble than you!"

Then I started to feel icky
Big grape bubble in my tum
I guess I should have listened to Vicky
And never swallowed my gum

MY SHADOW

My shadow follows me wherever I go
No matter how I try to escape or hard the wind blows

I can't outrun it, I cannot hide
It's always beneath me or right by my side

It's there when I'm happy, it's there when I'm sad
When I'm surprised or when I get mad

Well, I have a plan I know my shadow can't beat
I'll do it tonight, a little trick up my sleeve

It's finally time, tonight is the night
To get rid of my shadow, I'll just turn off the light!

WHAT THE PENCIL SAW

Today I dropped my pencil
It fell onto the floor
But when I bent down to pick it up
I kicked it toward the door

It rolled right past the doorway
And out into the hall
It went hurtling toward the bathroom
And swirled straight into a stall

I tripped and flushed the flusher
Straight up, the pencil popped
It flew back into the hallway
That had just been freshly mopped

I slipped on the wet floor
And got mop juice in my hair
I saw the pencil twirl and spin
As it cascaded down the stairs

It spiraled into the lunchroom
Past greasy food, so fried
The pencil jumped right over lunch
And capitulated itself outside

I rushed to catch it before the road
But it sure was hard to beat
That pencil fled the schoolyard
And dove right into the street

I looked left and I looked right
No cars anywhere around
So I pursued the pencil
As it made its way across town

The pencil crossed the big blue bridge
And took the bike path by the lake
The pencil pounced past many dogs
And bakery windows filled with cake

The pencil plunged past happy families
And the park where children play
Then the pencil took a sharp left turn
Swerving into my driveway!

It bounced up the stairs, past mom
Round the couch, to the office door
The pencil zipped and zapped so fast
Digging through our office drawer

The pencil grabbed a piece of paper
New thoughts and ideas to write and draw
After adventuring through the outside world
Isn't it great to see what the pencil saw?

LUNA'S LUNAR LULLABY

All the little birdies sang their songs during the day
But little Luna did things in a sort of different way
You see little Luna was a lullaby birdie
In the daytime, she was shy and not very wordy

But at night little Luna sang and wished on the moon
That everyone would soon hear her sweet lunar tune
So she whistled and sang all night long
When she was singing songs, nothing ever felt wrong

Just as the sun began to rise
Luna finally closed her eyes
But Luna was soon awoken, right there in her nest
Her parents said, "You can't sing at night! Nighttime is for rest!"

She cried and cried all day long
That night the moon did not get a wish or a song
She tossed and turned, and she could not sleep
Nothing seemed to work, not even counting sheep

All she wanted was to just sing one note
But she felt like she had a sad lump in her throat
She did not want to sing and make her parents mad
But without her song, the world seemed sad

Late that night she heard a faint little sound
A teensy squeaky noise coming from the ground
Luna said, "Hello? Is someone down there?"
"I'm Chippy the Chipmunk! Do you have a song to spare?"

Luna cried, "I don't sing anymore, sad to say."
Chippy gasped, "But your moonlit song makes my day!"
Luna was shocked, "You've heard me sing?"
"Every night for a month! It's my favorite thing!"

Chippy said, "I can't sleep, so I wander around -
One night I wished for help, as I scurried through town
Right after wishing I heard your sweet song
It sounded so nice, falling asleep did not take long!

I couldn't believe I ended up right at your tree
It was then I knew the moon had answered my wish for me!"
Luna said, "Chippy I'm happy for you-
But the moon didn't hear you. My song wasn't new"

"Oh, but Luna! That is where you are wrong!
I know the moon heard me and can also hear your song!"
Luna smiled and sang louder than ever before
Waking her parents and all the creatures down on the Earth's floor

Every creature below stopped and listened
The moon glowed brightly with light that glistened
Luna knew that the moon had heard her sweet song
And the moon had been listening all along

I CAUGHT A FALLING STAR

Last night I saw a shooting star
Sparkle and descend
I closed my eyes and made a wish
That I would make a friend

Suddenly the shooting star
Fell right into the park
So, I decided to take it home
To be my night light in the dark

I scooped it off the ground
After it fell down like a rocket
I had to ride my bike home
So I placed it in my pocket

When we got back to my house
We ran upstairs to play
But the star's fantastic shine and shimmer
Had been dulled to dusty gray

I asked it what was wrong
And tried to see if it was sick
I only got a small response
A tiny, faint, light flick

I wrapped the star in blankets
And read it my favorite book
I showed it all my toys
Better and better it started to look

I told the star my secrets
Shared my favorite movies too
I took the star outside
To see the sky from a better view

The star glowed brighter and brighter
As the days went on
We did everything together
We even mowed the lawn

We laughed, danced, and sang
We did makeovers and played
And the star lit up the night for me
I was no longer alone or afraid

I realized the friend I wished for
Was the star itself all along
And the star had also wished on me
To make it feel like it belonged

MISCHIEVOUS MINDY

Mischievous Mindy was always up to no good
When people said, "Don't touch that!" Mindy always would

Mischievous Mindy loved to break her parent's rules
She would get sent to her room, but she would break out with her tools

Mischievous Mindy was excellent at making booby traps
She would catch her little brother and her little doggy Scraps

Mischievous Mindy told her parents she brushed her teeth twice a day
But it turns out she didn't, so her teeth turned yellowish gray

Mischievous Mindy's parents told her never to be mean
But the next day at school, she was the meanest she's ever been

She bullied sweet Sally for having weird sparkly shoes
Sally cried so hard that her nose started to ooze

Sally told Mindy she had been sad now for a while
And this pair of sparkly shoes was something small that made her smile

Mischievous Mindy saw the look on Sally's face
And realized she did not want school to be a bad place

Mischievous Mindy apologized, and she even sort of cried
She said she loved Sally's shoes if they made her happy inside

That day Mindy learned, though it was a tough pill to swallow
That there really are some rules that you should always always follow

BUTTERFLY

Today I saw a butterfly
I watched it as it fluttered by
And as it fluttered and it flew
I dreamt what it would be like
If I could fly too

I'd make friends with birds and bees
I'd fly up higher than the trees
But one thing I must confess
I could not find my way home
Because I don't know my address

SPEAK UP!

In school, when my teacher asked a question
I would yell the answer out
But my teacher always shushed me
And told me not to shout

At choir practice, when we would sing
I would give it all I got
But the choir teacher told me
She would rather that I not

At the movie theater, I would chat
And clap so loud
But my parents told me to be quiet
So I would not bother the crowd

Use your inside voice! Be quiet!
Zip it! Don't holler! Hush!
Silence! Keep it down!
Button it up! Shush!

I was trained to be quite quiet
And use my inside voice
So I would only softly whisper
I did not have a choice

So over time, I just quit talking
Hardly ever said a word
I might have been seen
But I was hardly ever heard

Today my sister needed help
I told my parents, but they could not hear
If I'd learned to speak up when the moment was right
My sister wouldn't still be stuck up on that chandelier

HELLO?

I stood on a mountain, all alone
I went to the edge
And yelled into the unknown
"Hello?"

HELLO!

I heard a voice say
I couldn't believe it
Did it come from that way?
To see where it came from, I shouted, "good day!"

GOOD DAY!

"Hooray!"

HOORAY!

"YAY"

YAY!

Whatever I yelled out into the blue
The voice would repeat
And the voice seemed to move…
"Where are you?"

WHERE ARE YOU?

"Right here!"

RIGHT HERE!

"Who are you?"

WHO ARE YOU?

"Are you near?"

ARE YOU NEAR?

I looked all around

I searched everywhere
Up and down, and all over the ground
But there was nobody there to be found

I saw lots of trees and even geckos
And oh, I'm so embarrassed
I should have known from the get-go
But that voice was just my echo

ECHO

GWARGO THE ALIEN OCTOPUS

Gwargo, the alien octopus, was sent down to Earth
To observe human behavior and bring back something of worth
He saw all the strange and kooky things that humans do
Like sticking things together with this gloopy stuff called glue

He saw that after sleeping, humans made their beds
And when it was cold outside, they wore hats on top their heads
He saw that sometimes they were nice, and sometimes they were mean
And after playing outside, they would wash their hands clean

But he saw one special thing that put him in a trance
When this thing called "music" played, the humans would all "dance"
It seemed that dancing made them all get along and smile
It made their problems disappear… at least for a while

He had never heard music, but it made him feel happy
He listened to the beat, and his feet started to tappy
He wiggled his tentacles and waved them in the air
He danced like the humans, and he didn't have a care

He felt so excited to share dancing with the others
He wanted to dance with his sisters and his brothers
But they could not dance without music on the planet he called home
So, he recorded music on his cosmic record-a-phone!

Gwargo went back home to share his revelation
But the other aliens seemed to have a bit of hesitation
So Gwargo played the music to show them how it's done
He twisted and spun and showed them dancing was quite fun

Before he knew it, everyone in his little alien town
Was boogying and woogying and totally getting down
They all felt something happen deep inside their little heartys
Now every morning starts with alien dance parties!

www.ingramcontent.com/pod-product-compliance
Lightning Source LLC
Chambersburg PA
CBHW051753130826
49812CB00033B/1131
9789357442107